IT'S THAT SIMPLE

A User's Manual for Human Beings

MAVIS KARN

Foreword by
MICHAEL NEILL

Illustrated by
CELIA BOHLE

Caffeine for the Soul Press

It's That Simple

A User's Manual For Human Beings

By Mavis Karn

With a Foreword by Michael Neill

To Kids and Former Kids, Everywhere

Contents

Contents

Foreword by Michael Neill

"*Friendship is born at the moment when one person says to another, 'What, you too? I thought I was the only one.'*"

-C. S. Lewis

Have you ever had a person in your life who loved you so unconditionally you felt able to relax and be completely yourself around them?

If you've been fortunate enough to know someone like that, you'll recognize the feeling behind the fifteen simple yet thought-provoking letters in this book. If not, you may be about to have that experience for the very first time.

Mavis Karn has been one of those people for me for a number of years now. She's been my teacher, colleague, friend, and confidante. She's been my coach, sharing strategies during timeouts in the great game of life; she's also been my secret weapon in those moments when it felt like I was going into battle.

But while I would love to spend more words putting Mavis up on a pedestal, I know she would just hop off and remind me that we're all made of the same "god stuff" - and that when we remember that simple fact we have as much potential for happiness, joy, and impact as anyone in history. In fact, the only thing that makes one person seem more patient, kinder, or wiser than another is what they've come to see about who human beings really are and how perfectly well we're made.

There are so many simple truths packed into the pages of this little book that it's difficult for me to pick out my favorites, but here are a few that have made the biggest difference in my own life:

- Our feelings exist to teach us how to make better use of the gift of thought (*Letter One*)

- There is not one person on the planet who is not perfectly well made (*Letter Five*)

- Figuring things out is overrated (*Letter Nine*)

- We're not stuck with our habits, no matter
  how long we may have had them (*Letter Ten*)

- Worry is not a prerequisite to living a long
  and happy life (*Letter Eleven*)

If you've ever thought life would be a lot easier if it came with a user's manual, life's about to get a whole lot easier. So put up your feet, pour yourself a cup of your favorite beverage, and begin. The world you change might just be your own...

With all my love,
Michael Neill
Bestselling author of *The Inside-Out-Revolution* and *The Space Within*

Introduction

Hello dear reader,

Welcome to our book!

I am so glad you saw it and decided to see what it was about. I have never written a book before but I thought I might give it a try, mostly because I want to pass on what has turned out to be the best information I ever got in my life... the user's manual for human beings.

This is my definition of a human being:

We are pure intelligent energy in human form. We create our own experience of life and can realize we are doing it.

Over 40 years ago, I had the good fortune to be given this "user's manual" and as best I could, to begin passing it on to others. My work as a counselor/educator has given me many opportunities to do so.

Years after beginning to share the user's manual, out of a concern for the number of kids being lost to gang violence, I contacted an ex-professional football player, Oscar Reed, who had started a small agency in Minneapolis that offered much-needed attention to kids. He too was concerned with the amount of violence in the community, and along with his friend, Jim Marshall, was doing his best to educate them away from trouble. I passed the user's manual on to them, and we began to pass it on to kids in small, after-school groups.

This collaboration soon led us to a project that had us traveling for an hour every Sunday for two years to a juvenile prison, where we passed what we had learned on to incarcerated boys. We taught them who they really were, how well they were made, and how their minds worked. We gave them the user's manual for their own lives.

There were kids of multiple races, multiple different religions, and they were incarcerated for a wide range of offences.

We were pretty sure that if they got the user's manual and understood how well they were made, they could learn to see possibilities for themselves that were far beyond the limited visions and decisions that had brought them to prison. It turned out we were right about that.

At first, they were understandably wary of me, but gradually they gave me their attention and began understanding what we were saying: that they were whole, complete people who were born with the powerful tool of thought with which to create their own experience of their lives. They were, in addition, given the gift of senses in order for their thinking to come to life and guide them in the use of it.

In the end, there were so many wonderful stories that came out of that program I find it hard to choose just one, but this is one of my favorites:

Robbie was a seventeen-year-old boy from Chicago who came to the class for the first time. The kids and I were sitting in our circle as he told us his story. He, his mother, and his siblings lived in a public housing project that was well-known for the amount of criminal activity in and around it.

One day, when he was 10 or 11, he came home to an empty apartment - his family was gone. He hadn't seen them since, and had no idea where they were. He'd been on his own from that day forward, sleeping here and there, stealing food, getting caught, dealing, getting caught, burglarizing, getting caught. His explanation for having been left behind by his family was that "They left me 'cause I was a bad kid." That was, in his view, just a simple fact.

I was about to say something to him about his take on things when a boy sitting next to me said "Robbie, your momma didn't leave you 'cause you were no bad kid - - she left you ' cause she didn't know how to be a good momma". The rest of the kids spoke up in agreement. They assured him that he was good inside - that he was just doing the best he knew how and so was his momma.

I was stunned! They were so kind; so unexpectedly loving. There was no judgment for Robbie or his mom. I was so proud of them, and Robbie was speechless. It was truly awesome. I saw, in that moment, that a person's lifelong narrative about themselves could change in the face of love.

I don't mean to say that all of the boys magically turned their lives around in a split second. It doesn't mean they didn't bounce back and forth between embodying loving-kindness and being rowdy, noisy, profane kids. But they continued to experience many instances of love of the deepest kind, and that is very hard to forget or ignore.

Many of them did indeed transform their lives, some sooner than others. Some blew us off and went back to their old ways. But I like to think on some level, they were introduced to the truth about who they really were, and that the "seeds of truth" might lay dormant for a while but could begin to sprout at any moment.

As the 2 year-project came to an end, the last class was approaching and I became very emotional. I loved my time with them SO MUCH, and I loved them.

I felt like I wanted to bring them a gift in our last class, but what could I give to them that they all could use... socks? No. So I just sat down and wrote them a letter – the first letter you will read in this book. The letter found its way into the adult prison, and soon one of the inmates asked for permission to put it into the form of a poster.

Since that day, that poster has found its way all around the world and that letter has touched lives I could never have imagined intersecting with mine. I originally called it "The Secret", but now I tend to think about it as the whole user's manual for human beings in a nutshell.

While I have spent quite a bit of my professional life working with kids, one day, my son, Barry, joined me in passing on the user's manual to a small group of them. Barry was in his early twenties at the time and told them this story...

When I was about 16, I got a summer job at a church doing maintenance work. I was so excited because the job required me to carry around a large and really cool looking ring of keys hanging from my belt. There was a key for every room in the huge building. It took me quite a while to clean my assigned rooms, mostly because it took me forever to find which key fit which door. It wasn't until I'd been on the job for several days that the more experienced men on the job let me in on the joke: they took back the really cool looking but incredibly complicated ring of keys and gave me one "master key" that opened all the rooms. That was what it was like for me to learn about the user's manual. It was the one simple key to unlocking everything!

I hope this book helps you to see the simple truth about how well you are made. I hope it shows you that you can trust who you really are. It is a book of short letters I wrote with you in my mind, my dear fellow human being, and while you might want to read them in the order I've put them in, once you've gone through them once you can let this be a "sipping" book – a book you can pick up, read a page or two, take your time, keep what fits, and listen for the simple common sense of it all.

If you do find this information useful, you may one day find your own unique way to pass it on to others. If there is any sort of "master plan" in the universe, I would hope it includes that we are here to help each other live our truest selves.

"My words may seem too simple, but I say again, the truth is simple. Look for common sense, plain old-fashioned common sense."

Syd Banks

Letter One

Dear Kids (and former kids),

I have a secret to tell you. Nobody meant to keep it from you... it's just that's it's been one of those things that's so obvious that people couldn't see it... like looking all over for the key that you have in your hand.

The secret is that you are already a completely whole, perfect person. You are not damaged goods, you are not incomplete, you are not flawed, you are not unfinished, you do not need remodeling, fixing, polishing or major rehabilitation. You already have within you everything you need to live a wonderful life. You have common sense, wisdom, genius creativity, humor, and self-esteem. You are pure potential. You are missing nothing.

The only thing that can keep you from enjoying all that you already are is a thought. One thought. Your thought. Not someone else's thought. Your thought... Whatever thought you are thinking at the moment that feels more important to think than feeling grateful, alive, content, joyful, optimistic, loving and at peace... that's the only thing that's between you and happiness.

And guess who's in charge of your thinking? Guess who gets to decide where your attention goes? Guess who gets to write, produce, direct and star at the moment you're in the middle of? You! Just you. Not your past (stored thought), not the future (did you ever notice that it never, ever shows up?), not your parents (they all think their own thoughts), or your friends (ditto), or school or media or situations or circumstances or anything else. Just you.

Thinking is an awesome capability. Like any capability, it can be used whether as a tool or as a weapon against ourselves and others. And just like with any other tool, we can tell whether we're using it for or against ourselves by how it feels. When we think against ourselves or others, we get in trouble. When we don't, we usually stay out of trouble.

FEELINGS EXIST TO WARN US AWAY FROM USING OUR THINKING TO CREATE TROUBLE IN OUR LIVES AND TO GUIDE US BACK TO OUR

NATURAL, HEALTHY ABILITY TO LIVE OUR LIVES TO THE FULLEST.

So, please remember that your thoughts are not always telling you the truth. When we're in low moods, feeling down, our thoughts are not to be trusted… our IQ drops. When our thoughts pass and we lighten up, our thinking is once again creative, and positive… our IQ goes up. The only way you can feel badly about yourself and your life is if you think badly about them… it's up to you, every single minute you're alive. It's always up to you!

This is the best, most liberating secret I ever learned, and I want you to know it too.

With love,

Marie

"I laugh when I hear the fish in water is thirsty. I laugh when I hear that men go on pilgrimage to find God."

Kabir

Letter Two

OUR DIVINE ENGINEERING

Hello, dear reader,

Here I am again, writing another letter to kids and former kids. The first one is as true now as it was then. In the years since I first sat down to write it, I have learned more and more about the truth of it – about the simple perfection of how well we are made and how the understanding of that perfection is the difference between a life of love, compassion, kindness, security, and productivity versus a life of conflict, fear, resentment, and self-imposed limitations

So let's have a chat about the divine engineering of us.

Let's start with your hand.

There are twenty seven bones, twenty seven joints, thirty four muscles, over a hundred ligaments and tendons, and an astronomical number of blood vessels and nerves in the human hand - and most of us have two of them!

Scientists continue to try to create robotic hands that are as useful and efficient as the human hand, so you can see what a complicated task that must be.

Take a moment to make a fist and squeeze it really tight.

What uses can you make of your hand when it's clenched tightly like this? Punch? Pound? Threaten? Gesture?

A clenched fist can occasionally be useful, but it is almost always uncomfortable and often causes pain both to yourself and others.

What can you do with your hand when it is unclenched is an entirely different matter. You can feed yourself, dress yourself, build things, fix things, play instruments, play games, draw, paint, pick things up, put them down, speak sign language, and pet your pets.

Who is in charge of how you use your hand?

YOU!!

Your hand does not go off and get into trouble by itself without your intention or permission.

It is the same with your mind. When your thinking is clenched (angry, reactive, fearful, jealous, judgmental, insecure, etc.), it causes stress, limitation, conflict, and often results in destructive behavior.

When your mind is calm and clear, you are naturally creative, kind, compassionate, smarter, wiser, and much more able to avoid conflict and find solutions.

Can you see that it's that simple? Can you see that we experience all emotions as physical sensations?

Sensations guide us in the use of our remarkable tools, be it our own hands or our own thinking...

- Just like a sensation lets us know if our shoes fit.

- Just like a sensation lets us know if we should put a coat on or take it off

- Just like a sensation tells us if we're thirsty or hungry or tired.

- Just like a sensation lets us know if we're walking on smooth or rough ground, wet or dry, slippery or not, if we are walking uphill or downhill.

- Just like a sensation informs us whether sound is too loud, too soft, or just right.

- Just like a sensation tells us if food is spoiled or fresh.

- Just like a sensation alerts us to the fact we've sat in the same position too long.

- Just like a sensation tells us the difference between being hit or being hugged.

Can you see how *all* sensation has our back? It's all on our side!

WOW!

I'll write again soon. I promise.

Love,

Marie

"All life is made of
the same elements,
in billions of
different
configurations.
We are made of the
same stuff as stars -
we are stardust!"

Carl Sagan

Letter Three

A STORY ABOUT BUSES

Here I am again, dear reader!

In one way, the story I'm about to tell you never happened. But in another way, it's happening every minute of every day for all of us...

I was brought up in a family that, for as far back as I can remember, shared the belief that any time a bus came by, we had to get on it and ride it to wherever it was going. We didn't know that we believed that – it was simply a way of life to us that we never questioned. I, along with the rest of my family, spent most of my waking hours on buses, spent most of my money on bus fares, and found myself frequently lost and wandering around places I didn't want to be and wondering why I was always so tired and joyless and confused.

One morning, as I was standing at the bus stop ready for another long day of bus rides ahead, a man I'd never seen before said to me, "Excuse me, but why are you always riding the busses?"

"Well", I said, somewhat defensively, "everyone knows that's what buses are for. To ride. My whole family has always ridden them all day long – sometimes even all night long."

He looked at me as though I was the one who was strange.

"That's not what buses are for", he said. "They are for getting you where you want to go. Haven't you noticed that everyone doesn't always ride every bus?"

The man was beginning to annoy me with his peculiar ideas, so I ignored him and climbed on the very next bus that came along.

One day, while I was feeling particularly tired, frustrated, and a little bit hopeless about my life, I looked out the bus window and saw people walking, sitting, laughing, talking, and just simply enjoying themselves. I very much wanted to feel what they seemed to be feeling.

I decided to see what would happen if I, just once, let the bus go by without getting on it. As I sat at the bus stop, I saw the next bus coming, and I looked around nervously to see if anyone from my family could see me. Instead of getting on, I let the bus go by. It was a very strange, unfamiliar and somewhat confusing sensation.

Then another bus came by, and another, and another, but I let them all go by! It was still awkward and unfamiliar, but it was getting easier and easier. Soon, I noticed that I still had the money I would have spent on those buses, and I hadn't gotten lost once all day. In fact, the more buses I didn't get on, the more energy I had.

Then along came a bus that was on its way to where I wanted to go so I jumped on. I got off at my destination and all of a sudden I knew that the stranger at the bus stop had been right:

Buses are just there to help me get where I want to go, and I don't have to ride the ones that will get me lost or take me to places I don't want to be.

There was nothing wrong with me, or even with buses. I had just believed something that turned out to be untrue.

Happy travels!

Love,

Marie

"No matter what happens, you never, ever run out of chances to change your mind."

Anonymous

Letter Four

MAKING PEACE WITH ANY FEELING

Dear reader,

Here I am again!

Have you ever wondered what to do when you're feeling anxious, upset, scared, or any other feeling you don't want to feel at the moment?

If so, I think you might enjoy this little exercise. It just takes a few minutes and once you get the hang of it it's portable - you can do it anywhere, any time:

1. Find a chair, sit down, and let yourself relax.
2. Close your eyes.
3. Create a feeling of anxiety (just a little)
4. Notice where in your body you feel the anxiety and put your hand there.

5. Put your attention on that sensation and follow it as though it were leading you somewhere. (If your attention wanders, just bring it back to the sensations.)

As you do these simple things, you will notice the tight, tense sensations begin to dissipate and fade away, leading to a natural sense of calm. That feeling of calm is what it feels like to just be you - the you that is and has always been there underneath the noise of your thinking and the temporary discomfort of sensation.

The science is simple. In order to put your attention on the stressful sensation, you had to take your attention off of the thinking that produced the stress. That's all the sensation wanted! That's what it's for! What an app!

The moral of the story is that you can't sneak a thought past your body, and your body is made to handle any sensation no matter how uncomfortable it might seem.

It's good to get acquainted with yourself and your divine engineering, don't you think?

Love,

"What lies behind
us and what lies
ahead of us are tiny
matters compared
to what lies
within us."

Ralph Waldo Emerson

Letter Five

_____

A COMPLETELY WHOLE, PERFECT PERSON

Dear reader,

The user's manual assures us that we are already complete - that we have everything we need built into us from birth as a part of our divine engineering. In fact, since the day I first learned what's in the user's manual, I've never met or worked with a single human being who was broken.

I've met plenty of people who thought they were broken, some who could tell me where their brokenness came from, and still others who showed me doctor's notes to certify the specific form their brokenness had taken. But in all that time, I've never met ONE PERSON who was not perfectly well made.

For example, I met a man yesterday who was very ill, sad, exhausted, and unable to see his way out of the heavy, dark place he found himself in. Besides being ill, he was also feeling the recent loss of a beloved sibling.

As I sat with him, I realized that I could feel him in my heart. It felt as though we were one person - that his being was also my being. I felt completely connected to him, like we were woven of the same fabric. It was a deep, loving, warm feeling of compassion.

What I did NOT feel was pity. I did NOT feel sorry for him. I did NOT worry about him. I did NOT try to cheer him up, give him advice, or try to fix him. I did NOT commiserate with him. (Definition of commiseration: agreeing to be miserable together.)

I haven't always understood the vast difference between compassion and pity. That lack of understanding led me to react to suffering as though the person was helpless or weak or incomplete or "less than". I would, without their permission, jump in and try to save them from their trouble - to solve their condition, to be their solution, or to be a hero.

How disrespectful!

How different it is to be able to see a fellow human being as an equal, as someone who is temporarily lost in a world of spinning, fearful thinking about their circumstances, just as I have been many times. How freeing it is to know that they are whole, complete, resilient fellow human beings who have just lost their way for a bit.

Here's a story about one of the first times I really got how true that is...

Across the street from my office is a beautiful urban park, full of gardens, ponds, fountains, a basketball court, etc. Whenever I have a few moments, I take a walk and check the work of the Volunteers of the Park and their latest projects.

One day, as I approached the brick walkway around a flower garden, I saw a young mother, pushing a stroller with a toddler in it. Hopping along in front of her was a little girl of about three, clutching a handful of flowers. Off to the side a few yards away, a man was sitting on a bench, bent over, staring at the ground. I imagined him to be homeless, surrounded by bags of belongings and looking despondent.

The little girl noticed him and stopped in her tracks. She stood there a moment and then walked over, reached out, and offered him the flowers. He looked at the flowers and tears rolled down his cheeks. She leaned in, patted his knee, and ran back to her mother. It took my breath away!

I may never have seen such a beautiful example of a human being's natural capacity for love and compassion.

That little girl is who we all are. She did not need to be taught kindness, respect for human dignity, or any of the other things we adults hope our kids will learn. Once you've seen the perfection of who all of us (including you) are, you can never truly forget it. I know I will never forget that little girl.

If I am truly going to follow the golden rule and treat others the way I wish to be treated, I just need to show up and be myself. From there, I can bear witness to their distress and suffering by listening deeply to them from the cleanest, clearest feeling I can find. If there is anything more to be done, it will occur to me to do it.

I recommend compassion. Try it on for size. My guess is that it will be a good fit for you.

Much Love,

Marie

"We are already
one. But we imagine
we are not. And
what we have to
recover is our
original unity. What
we have to be is
what we are."

Thomas Merton

Letter Six

THE SIMPLEST WAY TO MAKE A DIFFERENCE WITH ANYONE, ANYWHERE, ANY TIME

Here I am again, dear reader!

In our last letter, I shared how compassion is a natural part of our divine engineering. This time, I want to tell you about what compassion looks like in the real world, and to share the one simple thing you can do to elevate every interaction you engage in for the rest of your life.

If you want to make a positive difference with anyone, anywhere, at any time, all you need to do is listen to them. I mean *really* listen. I mean listen so deeply, so clearly, that you can hear what is in someone else's heart no matter what words they may be speaking.

Here's what I've learned in over eighty years on this wonderful planet:

Everyone could do with a good listening to.

I used to think I was a good listener because if called upon to do so, I could usually repeat back what someone said to me. In a workshop I attended many years ago, Sandra Krot, the wonderful woman facilitating it, showed me how mistaken I was. She taught me the value of setting aside all the noisy mental activity in my head in favor of concentrating on understanding what someone else is trying to convey to me.

Here's a little workshop you can conduct for yourself over the next few days...

For the purposes of our mini-workshop, let's say there are four ways that we habitually listen to one another:

1. Distracted

When we're distracted - by other people, background noise, or even the noise inside our own head - we barely hear the speaker. We're in a hurry, preoccupied with other things even as we pretend to be listening to the person speaking.

Little kids are geniuses at detecting distractions. They will crawl up on a parent's lap, take hold of their head, and turn it towards themselves until the parent has no choice but to show up fully.

2. Evaluating

As a professional counselor, I was trained to "listen" to someone by going into my head and analyzing, diagnosing, forming a response, and thinking of what advice to offer them. As an amateur human being, I learned to "listen" to people by going into my head and criticizing, forming a response, deciding whether I agreed with them or not, getting defensive, finishing their sentences, assuming I understood their words and phrases, and recalling similar stories about myself or that I'd heard about others, etc.

What I never actually learned how to do was just listen.

3. Paying Attention

The apparent opposite of distracted listening is "paying attention". Here, we are usually bearing down, concentrating, memorizing and/or taking notes, tightly focused, and urgent. This kind of listening is usually done to prepare for an exam, remember where you parked, getting directions, or to impress someone with what a good listener you are.

It can be useful if you're listening to gather information, but turns out not to be that helpful if you want to actually connect with another human being.

4. Deep Listening

Deep listening (or as some others have called it "quiet listening", "listening with nothing on your mind", or even "just listening") is easy, effortless, powerful, and highly impactful.

It simply requires a decision:

I am going to listen to this person until I can feel what they're trying to get across to me. I am going to listen until I can feel a golden cord of connection between them and me. What comes across may or may not have anything to do with what they are saying or how they are saying to it.

Here's all you need to do to complete the workshop. Over the next few days, every time you are interacting with anyone, notice how you are listening to them. That's all. Just notice.

Here are some questions to help you learn from your experiments...

- What did you notice about your listening? Could you tell when you were distracted? Evaluating? Paying attention? Connecting beyond the words? Did you go back and forth between them? Was it different with some people than with others?

- What was your experience like? Did you learn something useful about your habitual way of listening?

- Think of someone in your life who is (or was) a good listener. What does (did) it feel like to be listened to by that person? What does it feel like to not be listened to by someone? Which do you prefer? Which way would you like to listen to others going forward?

There is a wonderful side-effect to taking yourself through this workshop. Once you can notice how you're listening in real-time and decide how you want to listen going forward, begin listening to yourself the way you'd like to be listened to by others.

Try it - you just might love it!

"Listening is a loving practice. We have to listen so that we understand the suffering of others; we have to empty ourselves and leave space so we can listen well. Just by listening, we can alleviate a great deal of pain."

Thich Nhat Hanh

Letter Seven

ON SELF-ESTEEM

Hello, friend!

The dictionary defines "esteem" like this:

es·teem /ə'stēm/

noun

1. a sense of value

2. high regard

3. respect and admiration

4. judgement of worth

With that in mind, here's how I see "self-esteem". Self-esteem is a natural trait that we all have inside us. It is an organic knowing, before thought, that we are uniquely, beautifully possessed of. It is all that is essential. It is the truth of us.

Therefore, we cannot feel "less than" unless we have innocently and unknowingly learned to use the gift of thought to create a "less than" experience. How fortunate then that all is not lost! We are divinely engineered in a way that allows us to observe and become conscious of the moment we begin misusing thought as a weapon against ourselves. We can FEEL it.

It is very common for us humans to have picked up the habit of comparing ourselves to others (favorably or unfavorably) as a way of measuring our worth and value. But that doesn't make our evaluations true, or even accurate.

 In order to return to the truth of us, we need only sense the clenched feeling of having left our true self and wandered back into a habit of thought. It's that simple.

Be still. Let all the mental noise recede, settle down, and dissipate. That's the door back home. That's when you remember who you are and where you can experience the oneness with all things that people who have reclaimed their wisdom have been pointing to forever.

Much love,

"Life doesn't get any better than the simple experience of your own mental health."

Richard Carlson

Letter Eight

UNDERSTANDING MOODS

Dear Kids (and former kids),

This letter is being written during a time on our planet of a pandemic, great political upheaval, wars, and severe threats to planet earth and its ability to sustain life as we know it.

It's perfectly understandable if we feel overwhelmed, perpetually anxious, isolated, limited in what can be accomplished, and possibly hopeless. In other words, in a really, really low mood.

It would be understandable as well if we believed that these forces and conditions and circumstances surrounding us were the *cause* of our low moods, and that nothing could lift our spirits until those forces ceased to exist.

But even with everything that's going on in the world, the truth of the human experience still prevails. Conditions outside of us do not determine our internal experience of life. We do. No matter what.

Our moods are not created by anything other than our own thinking. Moods are human weather.

In Minnesota, where I live, we have a wide variety of weather. It ranges from freezing cold (40° - 50° below zero) to blazing heat (100° - 110°); from tornadoes and fierce straight-line winds that tear down trees, powerlines, and buildings, to calm cloudless days; from searing droughts to floods; from mountains of snow covering the entire state to to miles and miles of green and golden fields. Visitors marvel at the number of coats I have, each one suitable for whatever happens to be going on outside. I cannot control Minnesota weather, but I can dress for it.

So it is with our moods. The quality of our thinking fluctuates continually from negative to positive to neutral. We cannot control what thoughts show up in our heads, but we can notice our feelings and take them into account. We can dress appropriately for our human weather.

Because I am fortunate enough to have access to the user's manual, I don't trust my low mood thinking. I try not to speak from it or act on it - mostly because

I don't want to clean up the mess I'd make if I did. I know it's temporary, and I'll be smarter, wiser, and kinder again soon.

Isn't it a relief to know that even during trying times, the natural resilience of human beings is still available to us? We can trust it. We can catch ourselves misusing the tool of thought to create despair. We can be still and remind ourselves that our self-worth, creativity, and kindness towards ourselves and others are always near at hand. We are exactly who we need to be - always.

The most important question I can think to leave you with is simply this:

How do you want to feel RIGHT NOW?

Much Love,

"The birds may circle over your head but that does not mean you need to let them nest in your hair."

Marcus Aurelius

Letter Nine

FIGURING THINGS OUT IS OVERRATED

Hello again, dear reader!

For much of my life, whenever I found myself confused about something, I would do my best to try to figure it out. I would think and re-think, analyze, speculate, and process - usually to no avail. More often than not, when I finally gave up trying to figure it out, whatever I was confused about would clear up on its own.

That "clear up on its own" thing?

I'd like to have a chat about that.

It turns out that we human beings are so well made that we can come up with solutions and answers without having to search our memory banks for them. Instead, we can calm our minds, let go of our urgent searching, and allow the "brain dust" of our thinking to settle in order to make space for fresh insights, obvious answers, and right under our nose solutions.

There is an often told story of a truck driver who tried to go under a low bridge, but the truck was too tall and got stuck. Traffic began piling up behind him, and soon policemen, firefighters, and other truck drivers gathered around to try to help. A mechanic suggested they dismantle the truck; an engineer suggested they dismantle the bridge. But none of the solutions seemed feasible.

Finally, a little girl who was watching it all from the backseat of her mother's car said "Mommy, why don't they just let a little air out of the tires?" Genius!

I realize this may sound like it's all too simple, but I suggest you try it on for size. The next time you find yourself clenching up and and struggling to figure something out, do your best to relax, calm down, step away, and let go of the mental tug-of-war. Be open to the possibility that you will likely see what you need to see shortly after you stop trying to see it. It's not magic - it's just your divine engineering at play.

Much love,

Maria

"It was like this
sometimes:
sometimes a thing
was right in front of
him, so simple.
Yet it wasn't until he
closed his eyes and
shut down his
thinking that simple
became clear."

Kent Krueger

Letter Ten

ON NEEDS AND HABITS

Hello again, dear reader,

Today, let's talk a little bit about needs and habits.

My definition of "a need":

Something necessary or essential to existence

My definition of "a habit":

The learned tendency or disposition of thinking, acting, or behaving in a certain way, acquired by the repetition of such thinking, acting, or behaving

With those definitions in mind, the list of actual needs for human beings is pretty short: air, food, water, and shelter.

But have you ever noticed how our list of personal needs seems to grow longer when our moods are lower?

- A young child may demand more and more attention when they're tired and cranky.

- A teenager experiencing insecurity may obsess about their appearance and "need" more and better clothes, cosmetics, technology, etc.

- Discontented adults may spend more and more time and money collecting cars, homes, jewels, etc., but never ever feel as though they have enough.

- Unhappy people may want more and more alcohol, drugs, excessive food, etc. in order to numb their negative feelings.

All of these are simple and very common examples of our learned habit of creating false needs. These habits are not mental illnesses, incurable diseases, or proof of our brokenness. They are simply the innocent misuse of the gift of thought.

Some of these habits were learned so early in life that they feel completely normal - like ugly wallpaper we've gotten so used to we don't even notice it anymore.

I have a friend who told me that she had repeatedly tried to quit smoking but failed each time. She felt at the mercy of what she believed to be the most addictive substance in existence.

Then she came across the user's manual. She realized that she had unwittingly created a false need, and that her urgent, compelling thoughts about cigarettes were just that - thoughts. She found it clumsy but not particularly hard to remember that she was not sick and she was not her habit. She simply noticed her habitual thinking each time it showed up and let it pass by as best she could. Soon, the habit had begun to extinguish itself, and she no longer saw *any* substance as having power over her.

Our habits are not our enemy. We would be hard-pressed to get through any given hour without engaging in and relying upon habits like walking, talking, feeding ourselves, and using tools and technology. Manners, skills, proficiencies, and procedures are all habits we learn and use to live our lives with greater ease.

Our divine design enables us to develop habits that keep us from having to start over again from scratch every morning. Instead, we can learn about something, find a use for it, and practice (i.e. repeat) it for as long as it seems helpful.

But since we are human beings, and therefore free to use or misuse any of our abilities, including the ability to create and maintain habits, each one of us carry around some old outdated ones that no longer serve us. While habits like worry, fear, judgement, insecurity, hatred, dread, and self-loathing are certainly common, they are not in our best interests to continue to engage in.

Can you see how all our habits work in exactly the same way? They may be positive or negative, helpful or unhelpful, but they are *never* who we are.

We are not the thoughts we think, the actions we take, or the habits we get used to. We are the creator of those thoughts, the chooser of those actions, and the maintainer of those habits. We are amazing!

With love,

Marie

"My sense of responsibility is the ability to respond instead of the compulsion to react."

Stephen Levine

Letter Eleven

WHY WORRY DOESN'T WORK

Dear reader,

This may be one of the shortest letters I'm writing to you, but it may well prove to be one of the most helpful. I'll begin it with my definition of "worry":

Worry is the learned habit of frightening ourselves with our own imagination.

Worry seems to be one of the world's most popular useless habits, but I think we keep doing it for what we believe to be legitimate reasons:

1. We think worrying is preventative.

"If I worry about all possible disastrous outcomes, maybe they won't happen."

The Truth:

Worrying to prevent disaster works about as well as any other superstition, like not walking under ladders to avert bad luck or avoiding cracks to spare your mother's back.

2. We worry because we think it's the same as caring.

"Of course I worry about you - I love you!"

The Truth:

Caring is based in wisdom and loving-kindness; worry is based in fear.

3. We think worry is being responsible.

"If I don't worry, it means it doesn't matter to me what happens."

The Truth:

Worry interferes with and limits our ability to respond.

Here's a little exercise for you. You might want to write your answers down instead of trying to keep them in your head...

Make two lists:

- How do I feel and act when I'm worried?

- How do I feel and act when I'm not worried?

Now take a look at both lists side by side. What's your preference?

Does it make sense that the less we worry, the more we might feel the way we'd like to feel?

Does it make sense that worry might be optional?

Isn't that good to know?

Much love,

Marie

"Fear not."

Jesus

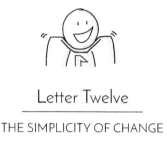

Letter Twelve

THE SIMPLICITY OF CHANGE

Hello, dear reader!

Many years ago, a professional sports team sent me one of their players who was always getting in fights in bars. He was a really, really good player, but they were afraid they were going to have to cut him because it was costing them money to repair the bars and all that that entailed.

He showed up in my office and took up half the room. He was huge, and he was upset, and he didn't really want to be there. But he also like making millions of dollars, so he stayed.

I started by asking him a few questions about why he thought he was there, and he started sharing stories about how when he went out to bars with his friends, people would come up to him and say all these godawful things about his mother and his sister and pretty much the worst stuff you can imagine.

It became obvious that in his world when someone disrespected you, you either did something noisy and violent in return or you would be seen as weak. He didn't see anything wrong with that – it just kind of made sense to him and seemed perfectly appropriate. But to me, it was pretty curious.

I'm a surprisingly big sports fan, so I had seen him play and knew how good he was at his job. I said to him, "Isn't there a lot of 'trash talking' that goes on before and after every play?"

He started telling me way more details about some of the trash talk than I wanted to hear, so I interrupted him to say, "Well, it doesn't look like trash talking bothers you when you're playing."

"That's right," he said proudly. "Nobody can get me off my game."

"So how come when you go into a bar and somebody trash talks you, you lose it?"

He got a funny look in his eye and he said quietly "Is that what they're doing?"

And I said "Well, I don't know, but what's the difference between what they're doing and what the players on the other team are doing?"

He thought about that for a few moments and said, "Oh, I can handle that."

Then he got up, said goodbye, and left my office.

It all happened so quickly that I was pretty sure he was just going to fall back into beating people up, so after a couple of weeks, I called the team to see how it was all going.

They said "What did you do to him? He's still playing like a mad man but off the field he's just a pussycat."

And I said, "I have no idea."

Which is true. I don't know why change can happen that quickly, but I do know that it's ordinary, not magic. It's a part of our incredible design.

With love,

Maria

"Do the best you can until you know better. Then when you know better, do better."

Maya Angelou

Letter Thirteen

IN PRAISE OF NOW

Dear reader,

Let's do some simple math regarding time. If the past is made of memory (stored thought) and the future is made of imagination (dreamed thought), then the only time that has any reality to it is NOW. Which means it is always NOW, it will never in your lifetime be any other time than NOW, and we can only ever experience NOW.

So if we are the experiencer - the creator of our own thought by thought experience of our life and the author of our every moment - the most important question we can ask ourselves is simply this:

How do you want to feel (experience) NOW?

We are often advised to "be present in the moment" as if there were actually any alternative available to us. For example, when I was a very young girl, my father was in the armed services in the war in Europe. One day someone mentioned it was already Tuesday where my dad was, so I asked if we could call him so he could tell us what happened. Then we'd get to know about it ahead of time. Everyone laughed, but no one explained to me why that plan wasn't likely to work out.

It took a few years, but I get it now. It is always the same NOW everywhere. It is always just NOW. And NOW is always enough. So why don't we just stay here and live from moment to moment?"

I suspect it's because like with most habits, leaving the present to hang out in the past or future seems reasonable to us. To begin highlighting the faulty thinking behind those reasons, I'd like to share some thoughts I have about "the past".

It seems to me that we don't really realize that the past doesn't even exist outside of our own minds. What we call "the past" is a collection of memories that, more often than not, are inaccurate and incomplete. It is a blend of spotty thinking, revised facts, selective editing, blatant falsehoods, and unconscious fantasies.

Our pasts are stories stored in our memory banks about the best we (and everyone else) knew to be possible at the time they happened. This is the simple truth. Nobody could do better until they knew better. It is also true of NOW. We are doing the best we know to be possible, moment by moment. And when we know better, we will do better.

I think it would be really, really helpful if we all understood that about ourselves and others. It explains everything. It is why we cannot have a better childhood, and it is why we need to stop telling ourselves we can't enjoy life NOW until some mythical moment in time when our pasts never happened.

The same thing is true about the future. For example, may years ago I was at a family gathering, sitting in a rocking chair with a relative's newborn daughter in my arms. It was a lovely, soothing feeling to just look at her and marvel at her perfect tininess.

I began overhearing some snippets of conversations nearby:

- "Won't it be nice when she sleeps through the night?"

- "Just wait until she starts smiling - that's the best!"

- "I bet you'll be glad when you can wear your regular clothes again!"

- "Won't she be lovely when she grows some hair?"

Unwittingly, everyone was creating subtle dissatisfaction with NOW by focusing on how much better things would be in an imaginary future. Then it occurred to me that I did the same thing on a regular basis, using phrases like "I can hardly wait until...", "Won't it be nice when...", "I wish ____ would be over so that ____ can start happening", etc.

Isn't that an interesting habit of using one's thinking?

Since NOW is the only time that actually exists, it seems a shame to waste it by always wanting to trade it for something better in an imaginary future.

If you are anything like me, keeping your attention on NOW has been an elusive task at times. But the good news is, leaving NOW to get lost in the remembered past or imagined future is just a habit. That means we can catch ourselves at it in any moment and come straight back home to NOW.

The more clearly I see this, the more I notice myself and others doing so naturally, without effort. I see that we were all born with the present moment as our default state, and just got slowly, innocently, incrementally educated away from hanging out there.

This is as true in our actions as it is in our thinking. There is an ancient Taoist concept known as "Wu Wei", which roughly translates as "effortless action" or "spontaneity".

This is the state of mind babies and small children exist in most of the time. It is also a good description of "the zone". Most athletes I have known, both personally and professionally, are well acquainted with "the zone", as are artists, musicians, scientists, writers, and anyone else who periodically finds themselves completely absorbed in something beyond themselves.

"The zone" has been described as a feeling of timelessness, a "no-thought" sensation, a sense of complete well-being and responsiveness where we have everything instantly available for the task at hand.

Most of us tend to believe that this seemingly magical state of flow is only available in a specific activity or set of circumstances, and even then only sporadically, appearing out of the blue when we least expect it. But what if "The zone" is portable? What if it's experienceable any time, anywhere by simply getting out of the way and allowing ourselves to fully experience whatever it is that we are doing NOW?

Can you see that means we are only ever one busy-headed moment away from being in "the zone" and experiencing flow NOW?

Could it be that simple?

Love,

Marie

"As you walk and eat and travel, be where you are. Otherwise, you will miss most of your life."

The Buddha

Letter Fourteen

YOUR NATURAL CREATIVITY

Hello reader,

Did you know that you are naturally creative?

I'd like to explain a bit about what I mean by that.

Here's the dictionary definition of the word "create":

cre·ate /krē'āt/

verb

1. to bring (something) into existence.
2. to give rise to
3. to originate

The intelligent energy at the heart of the universe is the source of everything we can see (the form) and everything we can sense (the formless). It is the creator of all of it - including us. Then we, in turn, get to be the creators of our own individual experience of this larger, created whole.

Isn't that amazing? What a perfect circle!

When my great-granddaughter was about 3, I was watching her as she rocked back and forth on her rocking horse. She apparently decided she wanted the horse to stop rocking, so she got off, walked over to the bookshelves, lugged a big book over to the horse, put it under the rockers, climbed back on, and just sat there, looking very pleased with herself for her creative solution.

However tempting it may be to just brag about my great-granddaughter, her story is a simple example of the inborn creativity in all of us getting the chance to come through.

Let's look at what that means for us in a down-to-earth, common sense, everyday sort of way.

Creativity is inarguably at work when we consider what has been 'brought into being' in terms of art, music, invention, architectures, and all the man-made wonders of the ancient and modern world. And we can see this same creativity at play in our own ability to create our every experience of life with the incredible tool of thought. By simply noticing how we're feeling from moment to moment, we can keep ourselves out of learned habits of creating misery and suffering while we show up in the world more of the time in the nicest feelings we can find.

As if that weren't enough, this same creative capacity can give rise to responses we´ve never thought of before:

- suddenly knowing the exact right thing to do/not do in a potentially dangerous situation

- coming out with an exact appropriate response to someone in their time of need

- offering up a simple, common-sense solution to a seemingly complex problem.

In other words, the creativity which made the world is always available inside us, offering up original, wise, common-sense solutions and real-time responsive guidance to help us navigate our day to day lives.

What an app!

With much love to a fellow artist,

"Maybe there are only three kinds of stories: those we live, those we tell, and those that help our souls fly upwards to a greater life."

Ben Okri

Letter Fifteen

ON LOVING KINDNESS AND SHINING EYES

Hello, dear reader –

I'd like to begin this letter with one of my favorite questions:

When was the last time you felt the way you wish you could feel all the time? What did it feel like?

In her book *Creating the Teachable Moment*, Darlene Stewart tells the story of her interaction with a young boy diagnosed with attention deficit disorder:

"When he forgot (to take his medicine) as he did today, he was a tornado in tennis shoes; windows shook when he passed. Now, slumped against the wall, he was unnaturally quiet. Looking at the defeated boy, my mood dropped too. From that state of mind, I had no techniques, no words of advice or encouragement; I felt like I'd said it all before, hundreds of times.

Not expecting an answer, I asked, "Danny, what in the world do you want?"

Without hesitation, Danny looked at me and said, "I want shining eyes."

A big hole opened in front of me.

"What do you mean?" I asked, already knowing the answer.

Danny said, "I want shining eyes. I want someone, when they see me, to get eyes that are soft and wet and shiny like they have light coming from behind. Shining eyes. That's what I want."

While on the one hand that's a beautiful story about a little boy who desperately wanted to experience love, it's also a story about a woman who *understood* that's what he wanted and was happy to give it to him - who was able to see past his behavior to who he really was.

We can all do that. We can all stop getting fooled by our own unhelpful habits and the unhelpful habits of others.

All Danny wanted was to be treated with loving kindness, even when he was misbehaving or in a low mood. And it turns out that loving kindness looks a lot like shining eyes. *How* you choose to be kind doesn't matter as much as *that* you choose.

Find that place in you that is naturally full of kindness, compassion, and grace and act from there. Any action taken from that place has a ripple effect we can't begin to imagine.

With loving kindness (and shining eyes),

Marie

"How wonderful it is that nobody need wait a single moment before starting to improve the world."

Anne Frank

Epilogue

Some final thoughts and reflections...

Here we are at the end of this little book letters. I hope you have had as wonderful a time reading them as I did writing them!

I have one final story and one more letter to write to you before we go...

One final story

Remember that group of kids I began working with back at the beginning of the book?

Fortunately, my colleagues and I had the chance to continue spending time with some of the kids in the group after they'd been released from the detention center back out into the world.

We were about to begin a reunion class with about 15 - 20 of them when one of the boys asked if he could talk first.

"Go ahead," I said.

He paused, looked around the room, and began pointing at each kid, naming them by their gang affiliation if they had one.

I felt a bit nervous about where he might be going with this, but I somehow knew to let him keep going.

Then he said, "In the past, most of you have been my enemies, but now, I have love for all of you."

There was a minute or two of silence and I found myself holding my breath, expecting a certain amount of embarrassment or discomfort from the other boys. But when they began talking, it was about what the world would be like if everyone knew what they now knew.

"There wouldn't be war!" said one. "No crime!" shared another. Someone shouted out "We wouldn't need jails!" A quieter voice said, "All babies would be loved." The one thing they all agreed on is that there would still be gangs, but they would be "gangs for good."

They spent the whole hour in that amazing conversation. Though my colleagues and I barely spoke, we were moved to tears. We had hoped for good results, but none of us could have imagined what we had just witnessed. Even having known about the user's manual for years, I had still underestimated what a bunch of ordinary kids could accomplish when they camc to scc that they weren't broken and came to understand how perfectly well they were made.

My dearest wish is that in reading these letters, you come to see how much you've been underestimating what one ordinary person who knows a bit about who they really are and how their mind works can accomplish. In other words, you - exactly as you are right NOW.

Which leads me to my final letter...

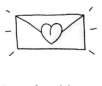

One final letter

My dear, dear reader,

Thank you so much for reading these letters. They were all meant for you, my sweet fellow human being!

Here are a few things I truly hope...

- I hope there has been something in them that has resonated with you at a very fundamental level. I hope there are at least a few ideas that feel worth hanging on to, especially the fact that you are magnificently made, divinely engineered, and already possessed of all you need. In short, that you are enough, exactly as you are.

- I hope that you find joy, and peace, and gratitude, and esteem for yourself and others in the simple understanding that you and everyone else are made of "god stuff".

- I hope that you've begun to notice that you are always feeling your thinking - and that that's a good thing!

- I hope it becomes more and more apparent to you that loving kindness is neither passive nor a sign of weakness - that we can be kind and loving and strong and tough, all at the same time.

I am now in the evening of my life, and I am so grateful that I got to realize for myself what I have attempted to pass on to you through these letters. I used to wish I had learned it all earlier, before I made this mistake or that one. But as I look back on my life, I can see that I learned it at exactly the right time for me.

Somehow I know that if you've made it this far, this is exactly the right time for you, too.

With all the love I can imagine,

Marie

"There is no situation that is not transformable. There is no person who is hopeless. There is no set of circumstances that cannot be turned about by ordinary human beings and their natural capacity for love of the deepest sort."

Desmond Tutu

Acknowledgements

In some ways, this little book is the story of a letter written with deep love to a group of beautiful kids in a juvenile detention center more than twenty years ago.

As the author of that letter, I would like to thank the kids that inspired it - - they taught me more about what's possible for us human beings than I ever imagined. They are all grown now, hopefully living lives that were helped by what the letter said to them. I continue to hold them in my heart and wish them well.

In addition, it was written with loving gratitude to Joe and Michael Bailey, Evelin Blad, Celia Bohle, Julia Carmen, Ida Davies, Barry Karn, Christopher Karn, Toby Karn, Wendy Karn, Sandra Krot, Azul Leguizamon, Jerry Lee, Kathy Marshall, Jim Marshall, Bill Mauzy, Michael Neill, Oscar Reed, Mary Roesler, Todd Roesler, Lynne Robertson, and Felix Thissen.

I also want to express my eternal gratitude for the remarkable conversations, guidance, and encouragement from two memorable human beings: Sydney Banks and Archbishop Desmond Tutu. They walked their talk, and I miss them.

"If your compassion does not include yourself, it is incomplete."

The Buddha

About the Author

Mavis Karn is a counselor/educator/consultant in private practice in St Paul, Minnesota. She is also a mother, grandmother, and great-grandmother.

Over the past 45+ years, she has spent her time working with individuals, families, schools, businesses, hospitals, agencies, prisons, athletes, and athletic teams, as well as mentoring and training other professionals.

maviskarn.net

Printed in Great Britain
by Amazon

18686742R00081